CW00502477

Ukulele In Six Weeks

How to Play Ukulele Chords Quickly and Easily
for Beginners, Kids, and Early Learners

MICAH BROOKS

WORSHIPHEART

PUBLISHING | EST. 1985

Also by Micah Brooks

The Guitar Authority Series:

Worship Guitar In Six Weeks:
A Complete Beginner's Guide to Learning
Rhythm Guitar for Christian Worship Music

42 Guitar Chords Everyone Should Know:
A Complete Step-By-Step Guide To Mastering
42 Of The Most Important Guitar Chords

Fast Guitar Chord Transitions:
A Beginner's Guide to Moving Quickly
Between Guitar Chords Like a Professional

Guitar Secrets Revealed:
Unconventional and Amazing Guitar Chords,
Professional Techniques, Capo Tricks,
Alternate Tunings, Head Math, Rhythm & More

Guitar Chord Flipbook: An Essential Acoustic and
Electric Guitar Chord Reference Manual
that Fits in your Guitar Case

Songbooks and Music:

Micah Brooks All Things New EP Songbook

Micah Brooks All Things New EP

The Piano Authority Series:

Piano Chords One (All Seven Natural Keys):
A Beginner's Guide To Simple Music Theory
and Playing Chords To Any Song Quickly

Piano Chords Two (All Flat and Sharp Keys):
A Beginner's Guide To Simple Music Theory
and Playing Chords To Any Song Quickly

Christian Books:

Forsaking All Others:
The book we wish we'd had when dating,
engaged, and in the early years of our marriage
to set us up for future success.

21 Day Character Challenge:
A Daily Devotional and Bible Reading Plan

Galatians: A Fresh, New Six Day
Bible Study and Commentary

Ephesians: A Fresh, New Six Day
Bible Study and Commentary

James: A Fresh, New Five Day
Bible Study and Commentary

Micah Brooks

Copyright Information

Published by WorshipHeart Publishing

Dedication

This book is dedicated to my sweet family. To my wife, Rochelle: we walk every step of our journey together. Your support means a blessed life for me. To our four kids: you make life fun, exhausting, and delightful. Thank you! I also dedicate this book to Dr. Linda Gilbert. Though you've recently gone to be with Jesus, your imprint of music on my life is indelible and lasting. Thank you for helping plant the seeds of music in my heart long ago. Those have been watered, cultivated, and are now blooming with many leaves and branches.

Micah Brooks

Contents

Introduction

Welcome!

Welcome to *Ukulele In Six Weeks*! I am excited that you've decided to learn to play the ukulele. It's thrilling to tell you that in six weeks you will certainly be able to do so. In fact, by week four you'll have all the chords you need to play just about every pop or worship song on the planet. Whether you're interested in the ukulele as your primary instrument or you'd like to use it as the first step in learning guitar, this is the right book for you!

How each week is structured

All six weeks begin by you learning at least one chord. We'll jump right in with chords because they are the lifeblood of the strummed stringed instrument (ukulele, guitar, mandolin, and so on). Chords are how you play songs.

After each week's set of chords you'll learn some information about your ukulele, like the parts from which it's made, or about the process of music that will help you to be successful. Don't skip over these sections, but focus the majority of your time playing and perfecting your chords.

End each week playing rhythm chart examples

At the end of each chapter are some rhythm chart examples to help you use the chords you've learned. I do not include popular songs or old nursery rhymes to learn in this book. The reason is two-fold. First, whichever artist may be popular today–like Taylor Swift–will be yesterday's news tomorrow. It's trivial to try to keep up with trendy music in an instruction manual like this. Also, nursery rhymes, like *Old MacDonald Had A Farm* are boring and annoying. I don't want to be the cause of that song getting stuck in your head! Second, I want you to use the internet to find the chords for the songs that *you* want to learn. You only need a search engine like Google, the name of the song you want to learn, and then the word "chords" after it. Hit "enter" and you now have access to millions of songs. See why I don't include them in this book? I want you to play the songs you love!

Let's jump into week one. Your first chord is C. Let's go!

WEEK ONE (1): C

What to expect week one

By the end of week one, you will be able to play your first chord. It's called C! Learn to tune your ukulele for the first time. Plus, discover the best ways to hold it. After learning C, you'll learn the names of the different parts of the uke if you ever need to replace a part. Then, you'll get to try out some practice exercises. Week one is fun, rewarding, and very manageable!

How to tune your ukulele

Tuning your ukulele to the right notes is the only step you must do before playing your first chord. You'll need to know how to find your tuning pegs found on the head of your uke. You'll learn the rest of the parts of your instrument at the end of this chapter. There is a full diagram at the end of this chapter.

Getting the correct tuning for your ukulele means turning your tuning pegs to reach the correct pitch or note. Most of the time you will tighten your tuning pegs, which makes the note tune upward in pitch.

A standard ukulele tunes to the notes G for the fourth [4G] string, C for the third [3C] string, E for the second [2E] string, and A for the first [1A] string. If you're able to find the notes on the piano, you can use the diagram below to help you strike the note on the piano and then wind your uke's tuning peg until you hear the same note sounding from both instruments.

Ukulele Tuning

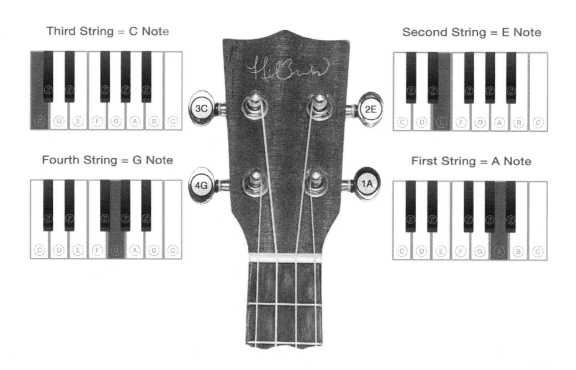

Third String = C Note

Second String = E Note

Fourth String = G Note

First String = A Note

Another option for tuning is to download a tuner app to your smart device. Search "ukulele tuner" in your device's app store. You'll likely find several free apps you can get. You'll strike a string on your ukulele, watch the tuning app to indicate whether you should wind or unwind your string (making the pitch go up or down), and then stop all winding when the desired tone on your uke has been reached.

Your first chord: C

Your first chord is C. It's simple and involves one finger. Begin by placing your index (1) finger on the third fret. Frets are metal pieces that are slightly raised above the neck. Frets are numbered based on the space in between each. Strum across all four strings to produce your C chord.

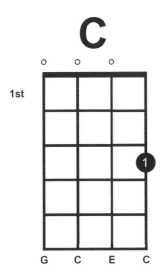

Press down firmly so that there is no buzzing sound from that first [A] string. If you feel like your contact isn't firm enough, pull your finger off the uke and try again. You want to develop strong finger muscles that produce clear sounding chords.

Congratulations! You know your first chord! You can now play the most important chord in your first key. The C chord is the root or fundamental chord for the key of C. As you learn more chords, this will make more sense. In short, the C chord sounds dominant to our ears and is the chord most often played in the key of C.

Special note: Each chord that you'll learn in this book strums across all four strings of your ukulele. While there are chords that use fewer strings, they aren't the fundamental chords with which you should begin.

While you've played C with your index (1) finger, it's important to learn how to play C with your ring (3) finger. Since we've only learned one chord so far it's not apparent, but the trick to playing ukulele well is to be able to transition between chords as quickly as possible. You'll need to play the C chord with your ring (3) finger to do that.

Notice below how we number each of the fingers on the fretting hand.

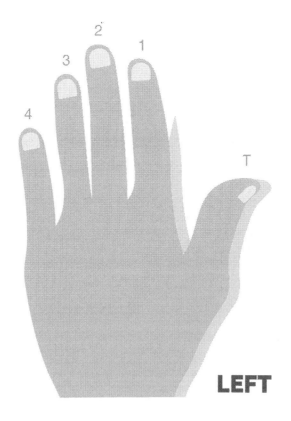

LEFT

It's time to use your ring (3) finger to fret your C chord. Practice taking your hand on and off the instrument and strumming all four strings over and over. Initially, you may find some discomfort from your fretting hand. Don't worry! This only lasts one to two weeks at most. Push through!

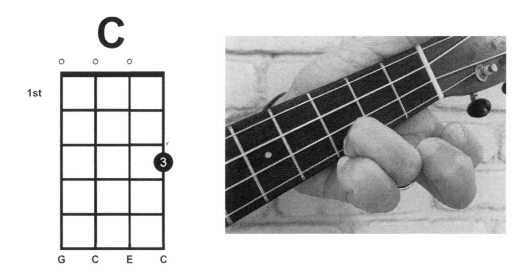

As you study this material, I believe you will notice that music is both artistic and mathematical. It utilizes both sides of the brain. God designed it to have a sense of free form and order all in one. Music is built upon twelve notes that repeat throughout the entire universe. Eight of these notes create an octave and only five or sometimes six of these are used in popular music. So, how can there be so many songs if only five notes were used to create them? That is the simple, yet complex nature of God's design.

I believe that talent is something God-given. Something that you discover. While skill is something that you have to develop. While God instills talent, you shape your skill through trial and error. This is called learning. Even the light bulb took over a thousand tries before Edison landed on its final invention.

Remember that anything worth doing takes time, effort, and perseverance. Recall this too as your fingers become sore or if you cannot master a chord on the first try. By the end of week one, you will have accomplished something of value. IMPORTANT: You can play the ukulele, it will just take time.

Parts Of The Ukulele

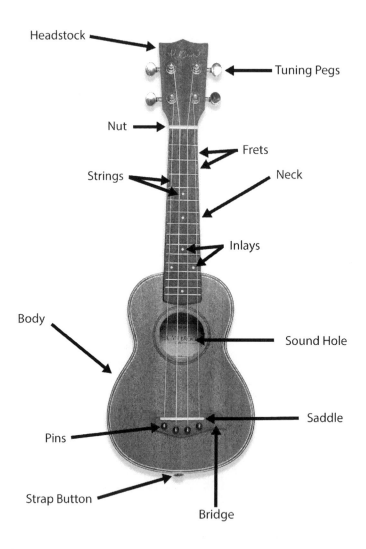

Headstock

Tuning Pegs

Nut

Frets

Strings

Neck

Inlays

Body

Sound Hole

Saddle

Pins

Strap Button

Bridge

Each part of your ukulele has a purpose. Much like our own bodies, each has a name. While you don't need to know where the wood from your ukulele was harvested, you should know the different parts. If your instrument were to break, you should know what to buy to fix it. Much like the human body, your ukulele has a head, or headstock, neck, and body. We will work head down.

Head

As you've already learned, the **head** (also called **headstock**) houses the **tuning pegs**. These are sometimes referred to as **tuners**. Your ukulele strings get wound together using the tuners. Pegs are what your fingers turn to increase or decrease pitch, which is the process of tuning.

The **nut** is at the bottom of the headstock and keeps the strings in place with small grooves and also slightly raised off the neck. Your nut is likely made of hard plastic. However, they can also be made from bone.

Neck

The **neck** is likely the longest part of your ukulele. It houses metal **frets** that live below the **strings** suspended over them. While you count frets by the metal parts, it's the space in between them where your fingers go. Pressing down the string in between frets creates a specific length that the string can vibrate. That vibration produces a certain pitch which is called a note. How's that for a short audio science lesson!

Your uke may or may not have small **inlays** at certain intervals on the neck. If you do have them, they exist to let you find neck fret positions quickly. They also give a special design element to the neck itself. In the diagram above, this ukulele has inlays on frets five, seven, ten, twelve, and fifteen.

Body

The **body** of a ukulele has the most parts. The **sound hole** is a uniquely designed hole cut to the right circumference to help sound build inside the body. The multiplying of sound through the sound hole is called resonance. You've likely noticed that acoustic instruments like the ukulele and the acoustic guitar have sound holes, but the electric guitar doesn't. Acoustic instruments amplify the loudness through physical sound waves bouncing around inside the body. Electric instruments amplify their sound through electricity and amplifier speakers. Each has unique sound properties.

Moving down the body, you'll find the **bridge**, **saddle**, and **pins**. All three parts form the bracing needed to keep your strings attached to your ukulele and at the right height above the neck. The pins hold the strings in place. Some ukuleles do not use pins. Rather, the strings are tied and knotted to the saddle. The saddle is the counterpart to the nut that is attached to the bottom of the neck. It is likely made of hard plastic but could be made from bone just like the nut. The bridge is likely the hardest piece of wood on your ukulele and has to endure the tension of the strings coming into the pin holes.

The final piece is the **strap button**. Your uke may not have one of these. Since the ukulele is such a light instrument, you may be able to hold it without needing a strap. If you do use a strap, it connects to the strap button on the bottom of the uke and tied to the neck at the top. I recommend not using a strap unless you find that you need it.

Last but certainly not least, use your rhythm chart examples

We discussed this in the introduction, but I haven't included specific songs to play in each chapter. You can use the internet to find songs that you love and want to learn. However, each chapter will have some rhythm chart examples and even some strumming patterns. There will be more to come on strumming patterns later. Please use these rhythm chart examples for practicing the chords you are learning. Plus, you'll be learning how to read a rhythm chart. Which is what professionals use in recording sessions and playing live as a quick way to learn a song. Charting is a simplified music notation.

Since you've learned the chord C so far, this week's rhythm chart example is simple. Downward strum your C chord four times in a row. Down strums are when your right strumming hand begins high and moves down across the strings.

Rhythm chart example using the C chord

Use down strums to play four measures of C and then end with a diamond–or whole note–C. This is a simple exercise, but making each down strum of the C chord sound as pristine as possible is the goal this week.

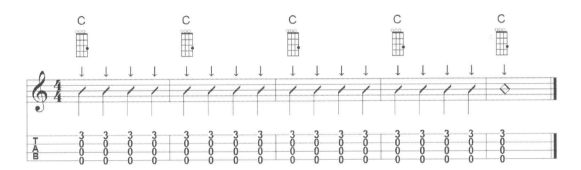

Micah Brooks

WEEK TWO (2): F

What to expect week two

Week two contains several important key things to learn. Before that, we'll discover our second chord, F. Then, we'll talk about the all-important way to transition quickly between chords. We'll finish with some professional-level secrets you'll need for strumming properly. As with each week, the final section has some practice rhythm chart examples for you to try out. This week you'll switch between two chords!

Your next chord: F

It's time to learn your next chord. It's the F chord. This is the second chord we are learning in the key of C. A key is simply a set of notes or chords that sound good together. C is the root or fundamental chord in the key. That's why its name is *the key of C*. The F is another chord in this key and it will sound good when played before or after C.

While C used only your ring (3) finger, the F chord uses two fingers. To form F, first, place your index (1) finger on the first fret of the second [E] string. Make sure you have strong contact with the fretboard and are in the middle of the frets. Last, add your middle (2) finger to the second fret of the fourth [G] string. Again, both fingers should be in

Mi

the middle of the frets, making strong contact. Also, confirm that you are not accidentally touching or muting the open strings around it. Strum downward across all four strings to sound your new F chord.

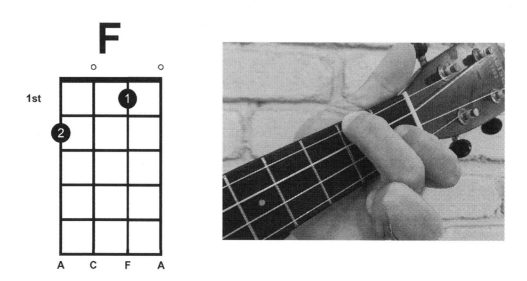

F

1st · ○ ○

A C F A

As you continue fretting this chord faster, attempt to move both fingers into position at the same time, using one simultaneous motion. Initially, you may not be able to do this quickly, but you will in time. That single motion will pay dividends down the musical road.

Transitioning between chords

Now that you have learned both the C and F chord it's time to begin to transition between the two. It may not be as apparent but transitioning between chords has a process and is as important as learning the chords themselves. Your goal should always be to move as many fingers in one motion as possible. And if there is a finger that doesn't need to move because it is shared between chords you'd like to use that finger as a pivot or anchor point with which your other fingers base themselves.

To move quickly between C to F, first play a C chord. Since there are no fingers that are shared between chords you won't have a pivot or anchor point allowing a finger to stay on the ukulele. This transition begins with your wrist twisting forward. Allow your middle (2) finger to lead the way while your index (1) finger is directly following your middle (2) finger. Now place both onto their spots on your uke to form the F chord. Make this transition over and over.

Getting back to C is simply the reverse of getting to F. Begin with the wrist roll. Take off your middle (2) and index (1) fingers in the same motion that your ring (3) finger moves into place for the C chord.

Practice going to and from C to F for five minutes each day this week. Use the rhythm chart examples to help.

Muscle Memory

One Sunday afternoon while I was dozing in and out of sleep during a nap I awoke just enough to hear a golfer on television speak about how it takes 21 days to change his golf grip. Even if he only wants to make a slight adjustment, due to muscle memory and the way our brains achieve things, we have to do things repeatedly before mastery. There's no way to cheat or shorten that time either.

As you learn your chords, practice does make perfect. Do your best to not get frustrated if you fail your first day or so with any new chord. Think longer term. If you can't accomplish a movement after 21 days then you can be frustrated and take up the harmonica or some other instrument. Again, practice makes perfect and it's non-negotiable.

Strumming

Strumming is the act of running your fingers (or pick/object) across multiple strings simultaneously. That can be across two or all four strings. Strumming, as opposed to picking, as we'll see next, is a motion you want to do well. Being a consistent strummer is far better than being an inconsistent one. It takes a lot of practice to keep your elbow in the correct position while moving the arm in a steady motion.

Were you to play guitar we'd be talking about using a guitar pick to strum. While you can use a pick on a ukulele you'll mainly see ukulele players using only their index finger. We will begin learning to strum properly with only the finger. In next week's chapter, we will talk about how to use a pick.

First, we will work on the *down strum* by placing the index (1) finger of your right hand on the fourth [G] string and run it through the first [A] string. Practice by playing four strums as consistently as possible. Precision is key to being a great strummer. Proper technique should look like you are wringing out your hand if it were wet.

After you've mastered the down strum, practice the *up strum*. It's like the down strum but reversed, beginning with the first [A] string and pulling upwards to the fourth [G] string. The up strum is harder to perform consistently. It takes more practice.

A little strumming secret

Special note about strumming: decades ago a friend told me a secret that changed my strumming life forever. The secret: when playing most rhythms, play as many down strums as possible. Use up strums sparingly and only as accents. Down strums are more dominant sounding and bring better force. All in all, the down strum is king.

Rhythm chart examples using the C and F chords

Transition between C and F in each measure of this exercise. Try to be as consistent in your timing as you can.

C Chord Rhythm Example

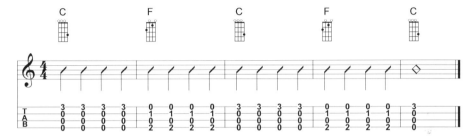

This exercise is similar to the last, but now transition C to F after two beats rather than every measure. This is tougher, but the goal is to stay consistent in your timing.

C Chord Rhythm Example

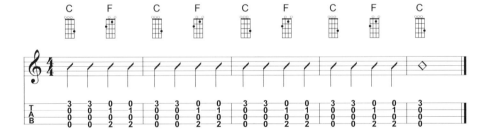

Micah Brooks

WEEK THREE (3): Am & Dm

What to expect week three

In week three, you'll learn your first minor chord–more on that to come first. You'll learn the Am and Dm chords. After learning those two, we'll talk about whether you'll need a ukulele strap or not. Then, we'll discuss plastic uke picks and the difference between picking with one or using your fingers to pluck strings. Finish with some rhythm chart examples now using four different chords!

Minor versus major chords

I've got some great news for you! The first chord, Am, that we'll learn only uses one finger. Before we launch into this one, let's talk about how to say the name of this chord. It would be natural to call this chord either the word *am* or to say "A" and then the letter "m". However, anytime that you see a chord with multiple letters it doesn't create a word. Rather, look at the capital letter and then any lower case letters that follow as two separate parts. The chord Am is said as, "A minor".

The capital A in this chord signifies that it's the A chord. The minor, which is abbreviated to a lowercase *m*, is a modifier to the A chord. If you were to see an A chord with nothing following the letters, you are to assume it's an A *major*. You've already learned, C and F. They are major chords. Major chords are solid sounding and I typically teach my students that they sound happy. Minor chords, on the other hand, flatten one of the happy notes–the third note of the scale–for its sadder sounding flattened third note. I'm not going to dive into music theory any more than this here. I have other books for down the road that have more to do with music theory. Suffice it to say here that major chords tend to sound happier, while their counterpart minor chords sound sad. You're about to learn your first minor chord. I bet you'll hear what I'm talking about!

Am

The Am chord is very easy to build. You only need to place your middle (2) finger onto the second fret of the fourth [G] string. Strum across all four strings.

It's important to note that you can also transition easily to Am from the F chord you already know. Fret your F. You have both your middle (2) and index (1) fingers on the ukulele. Now remove your index (1) finger. You've transitioned to an Am! Now transition back.

Am

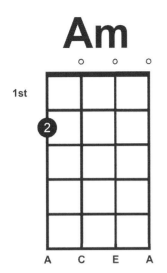

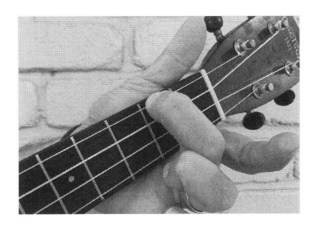

Dm chord

Dm is our first chord using three fingers. Building it from scratch may be tough, but I'll show you a shortcut after you learn the step-by-step method. First, place your middle (2) finger onto the second fret of the fourth [G] string. Next, add your ring (3) finger to the second fret of the third [C] string. Last, place your index (1) finger onto the first fret of the second [E] string. Strum all four strings.

So, what about that shortcut? Dm looks almost exactly like the F chord. The only difference is that you add the ring (3) finger. The shortcut is that you've already developed the muscle memory to add both your middle (2) and index (1) fingers for the F in one motion. Now, use that muscle memory, but add the ring (3) finger to create Dm. It's nearly the same motion, but one another finger joins in.

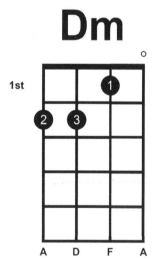

Ukulele Straps

If you'd like to stand and perform but the ukulele is either too heavy or odd-shaped to hold, you should consider adding a strap. Ukulele straps are often made of leather or polyester and are long strips of material that connect to the top of the neck and lower body. Because straps come in various designs and materials, there is no right or wrong choice. It's about your preference. I've seen people use shoe strings as straps. The main thing is that the strap is secure and holds the ukulele well. You don't want your uke to fall to the ground and break.

If your ukulele didn't come with a strap button installed on the bottom of your instrument, you may consider having one installed by a technician at your local music shop. I would not attempt to add one yourself because it involves drilling a hole into your uke.

Uke Picks

Ukulele picks are usually small, thin pieces of hard plastic designed to fit in your right thumb and index finger and used to strike the strings. Picks come in tons of different shapes, sizes and textures. I recommend purchasing a bag of *light*, plastic picks. As you progress on your uke, you can try out different kinds of picks. Harder picks will make the sound louder and brighter. Softer picks will make it quieter and milder. You should experiment.

Picking

Picking, unlike strumming, is about using a pick to play individual strings, rather than strumming them all at once. While some notes will carry over while picking, it's a unique sound. Begin by picking one string at a time. You can then alternate strings or even do high then low then middle. As you learn future chords, picking will come in handy.

Fingerpicking

Fingerpicking is the most difficult way to play consistently. While I won't go into great detail here, you make your hand into a claw-like shape, and then, as though each of your fingers is a pick, you pluck the strings individually. It's hard to stay consistent while fingerpicking as a beginner player. Most of your attention must be placed on your left hand that's shaping the chords. While fingerpicking, your right hand also needs your attention. You'll need to know your chords very well before you can focus more on your right hand.

Rhythm chart examples using the C, F, Am, and Dm chords

In this first example, let's play C to Am. Also, begin alternating up and down strums each time.

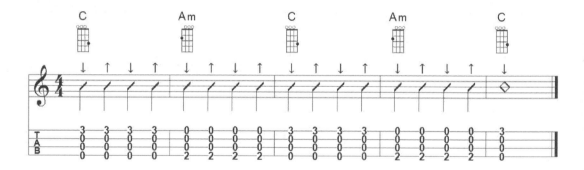

Next, add the Am chord to our C and F exercise.

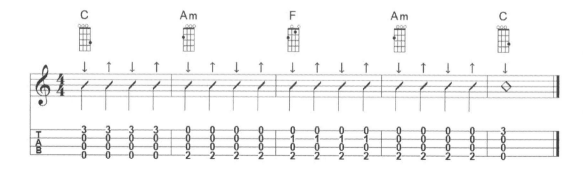

This time, we are going to add the Dm chord to our C and F exercise.

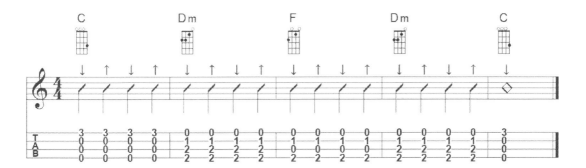

Last, let's use all four chords in one progression. Since this is more complicated, switch back to down strums only.

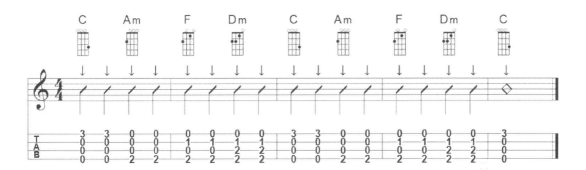

Micah Brooks

WEEK FOUR (4): G

What to expect week four

You've made it to the end of the month! Week four is a perfect capstone to the last few weeks of the ukulele! This week you'll learn one of the most important chords, G. It's the first chord that lends itself to the guitar most closely. You'll also find out about how to use a metronome–both physical and an app. Plus, you'll discover one of the greatest tools to be able to play in any key. You'll finish with some rhythm chart examples that use every chord you'll need to know in the key of C.

G chord

You're ready for the last chord in the key of C. You'll be learning G. It's likely going to be tougher at first than some of the others, but you'll get the hang of it.

First, place your index (1) finger onto the second fret of the third [C] string. Next, add your ring (3) finger to the third fret of the second [E] string. Last, and yes it's going to be a tight squeeze, place your middle (2) finger onto the second fret of the first [A] string. Strum across all four strings to play G.

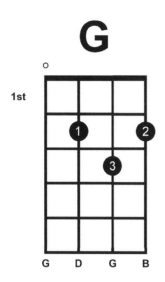

The G chord is interesting if you plan to transition to the guitar one day. The G finger shape on the ukulele looks identical to the D chord finger shape on the guitar. You'll already know one of the guitar chords when you begin learning that instrument! It's why beginning first on ukulele has so many benefits when transitioning to the guitar.

Metronome

We need to speak about a few pieces of gear you may add to your ukulele gig bag. A metronome is both loved and hated by professional musicians. A metronome is a device that keeps perfect rhythmic time. The metronome creates click sounds that are on beats 1, 2, 3, and 4. The musician or band attempts to stay in perfect step with it. It's very important as you learn to play ukulele that you consistently play with a metronome. The better you are with a metronome the better you will play without one. Some of the best musicians in the world play with close to perfect timing. I believe that it separates professionals from those who aren't. You can buy a physical metronome from your local music store or online. If you have a smartphone, you can download an app and always have your *met* with you at all times!

Understanding The Capo

The capo is among the mightiest of tools. A capo is a device used to raise the pitch of all the strings it lays across. For instance, playing a C without a capo will sound a C chord. If you put a capo across the entire 2nd fret and play that same C shape, you now have moved everything up two frets and you're playing a D, but using the C chord fingering. This is useful for two reasons. Sometimes playing the C chord shape is easier. The other reason is that the top note being played is the tonic note (or the root note) instead of the fifth note in the scale, like when using a D shape. You will be able to hear the difference. There are times when having the root note on top will make the most sense, especially if the melody being sung is the root as well. Forgive the little bit of music theory. My point being, the capo is an awesome tool!

Please don't let anyone ever tell you that using a capo is like a bicycle that has training wheels. Those people never had a proper understanding of how powerful a tool it can be. Some of the greatest players use capos as part of their signature sound. The Beatles' song "Here Comes The Sun" is played with a capo on the seventh fret of the guitar. Try out a capo on your uke!

Rhythm chart examples using all chords, now including G

We'll begin with a simple progression using G. Notice the new strumming pattern with two down and then two up strums.

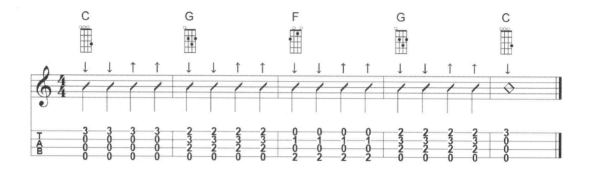

This exercise uses all five chords. Continue the strumming pattern as before: two down and then two up strums.

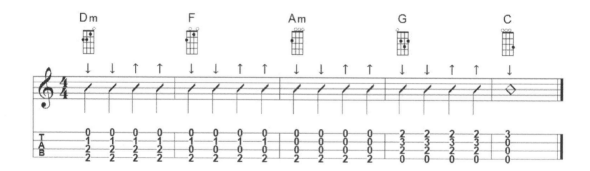

The final exercise uses all five chords but moves quickly between them. For simplicity's sake, use only down strums so that you can focus on making sure each chord sounds correct.

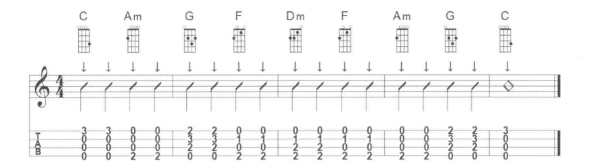

WEEK FIVE (5): D & Em

What to expect week five

Week five is another important step in your ukulele journey. You'll certainly learn new chords: D and Em. But, you'll also step away from the key of C and move to a brand new key. Plus, we'll walk through how to buy and put on brand new uke strings. I've included a special string changing secret you'll be glad to know. Finally, you'll finish with some new rhythm chart examples in this new key.

Welcome to the key of G

To this point, you've been using the key of C as the backbone for your playing. It's time to branch out into a new key. Today, we'll learn several chords in the key of G. You already know many of the ones you'll need!

The root or fundamental chord in this new key is G. You learned it in the last chapter. Instead of most of our exercises beginning with C, they will now use the root chord G.

We've worked to learn G, C, and Am. Each is an important chord in this new key. Now, you may wonder how some of the same chords are in two different keys. It's because the keys of G and C are relative to one another. Being a relative key means that they share several of the same chords. However, there are a few chords—the two you are about to learn—that are not in the key of C. They will help to distinguish the different sound of the two keys. You'll be able to hear it right away.

D Chord

The D chord uses three fingers you'll use to form a tight package. Begin by placing your index (1) finger onto the second fret of the fourth [G] string. Next, add your middle (2) finger to the second fret of the third [C] string. Last, squeeze your ring (3) finger onto the second fret of the second [E] string. Leave the first [A] string open. Strum all four strings.

You may need to adjust your wrist angle to keep all three fingers on the second fret. D typically takes a full week of practice before it becomes natural.

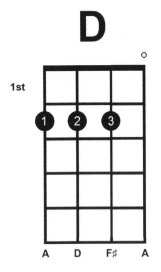

Em Chord

We only need to learn one more important chord in the key of G and we've got them all! The Em is another three-finger chord. Begin by placing your ring (3) finger on the fourth fret of the third [C] string. Next, add your middle (2) finger to the third fret of the second [E] string. Last, place your index (1) finger onto the second fret of the first [A] string. Strum all four strings. Begin with the open fourth [G] string.

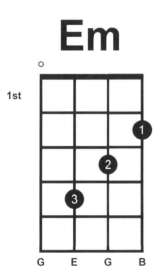

Choosing The Right Strings

Ukulele strings are the lifeblood of the instrument. They are normally made of soft nylon. Nylon is a type of plastic that resonates sound while holding strong tension. As you touch your strings, your fingers leave an acid residue which builds up over time. That residue causes the strings to become dull. You can feel a string to tell it has built up too much residue. Which means it's time to change strings. Depending on how often you play, that could mean you need to change your strings each month or as little as every six months. I'd say to not let your strings go longer than half a year.

You'll need to buy strings that are the proper length for the type of ukulele you own. Most beginner ukuleles are either soprano (the smallest) or concert (second smallest) length. Tenor and baritone ukuleles are larger, thus their necks are longer. Make sure that you search for strings that match the style uke you own.

While there may seem to be a hundred different brands and styles, choose a package or two of strings that meet your budget. A normal package should cost $6-$13.

How To Change Strings

Changing your strings is a skill to acquire. Yes, the store where you buy your strings will put them on for you, but they usually charge for that. Plus, when you change your strings you get to confirm that there aren't any new chips in the body of your uke. You identify any problems that have arisen. Also, you get to clean your ukulele. The shop isn't going to take near as much care for your instrument as you will.

To replace old strings with new ones, I typically follow this method and order. You can attempt other methods, but this is what I and some other professionals do.

First, remove the old strings. Do this by loosening the tuning pegs to the point where the string you want to be released can be pulled from its hole. I like to loosen all four strings from the headstock before removing them from the body. Once all strings are off, throw them away. They are old, used, and not worth keeping. Not even as spares. Most music stores sell individual new strings if you feel you need to have some spares. Old strings are stretched out and often covered in finger residue. They are spent. Throw them out!

Next, I clean the body and neck. I use cleaner or polish for the body, back of the neck, and headstock, but not the front of the neck. Make sure you remove all fingerprints and any unwanted residue off your uke. For the neck, I use ukulele-specific lemon oil. It refreshes the wood of the neck while still cleaning your frets. Lastly, I take compressed spray air (often used to clean electronics) to spray out any dust in the chamber of the body. When dust settles inside the body, it causes sound to vibrate in a different way than the ukulele was designed to thus changing or dampening its tone.

After you've sufficiently cleaned your uke, add your new strings. I recommend beginning with the thickest string [G4]. Many ukuleles have a tooth-like pin that needs to be pushed back in after you've inserted the ball bottom of the new string. Once in place, you should be able to stretch the string the entire length of the neck. Put the end of the string into the first hole on the left side of the tuner area on the headstock. I recommend making sure that as you begin turning the tuning peg the string is wound so that it moves the end of the string toward the middle of the headstock. This is rather than having the string wind toward the outside. In other words, the fourth and third strings should wind counterclockwise and the second and first should wind clockwise. If all tuning pegs are on one side of the headstock, I still recommend winding to the center of the neck.

A secret that I learned a long time ago about how to wind your strings so that they tightly hold –and stay in tune–is to let the end of the wound string first go UNDER the string being tuned. After the string has been under once, make the remaining turns go OVER the string being tuned. It creates a type of locking mechanism.

Repeat the steps above for all remaining strings. You should now have all new strings on your ukulele. Congratulations!

You'll need to do a few final steps before you are ready to tune up. First, you'll need to stretch out your new strings. This gets any leftover loose slack out of the strings at the headstock. It also helps the strings begin to balance. They came from the factory pretty rigid. To stretch your strings, begin by pulling them off the neck about 1-2 inches. Be safe! You want to stretch them at three-second intervals three times, releasing the string in between.

After you have sufficiently stretched your strings, it will be time to cut the ends of the strings that are still hanging off at the headstock. Be careful when using wire cutters or sharp scissors. Also, make sure you are cutting off the string excess and not the actual string that should remain. I have made that mistake before and it's not fun.

Rhythm chart examples using your new D and Em chords

In this first example, we'll use both of our new chords and also the G. Practice alternating down and up strums.

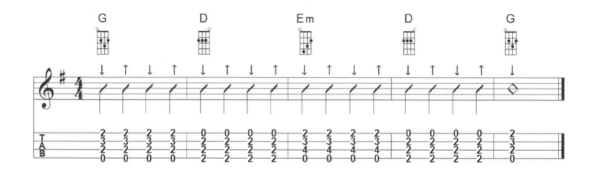

Now, we'll use a progression using each of the chords in the key of G that we've learned. Only use down strums this time.

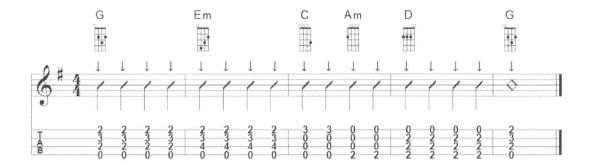

In this final exercise, we'll use all the chords in the key of G while transitioning between each quickly. Continue to use down strums for this exercise.

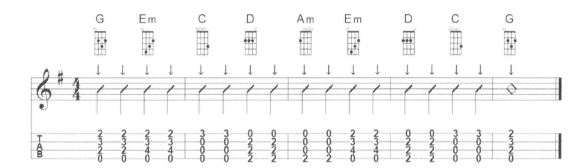

WEEK SIX (6): A & Bm

What to expect week six

You've made it to week six! This is wonderful! You're about to launch into your last and final key you need to know within the scope of this book. You'll learn the easy chord, A, and the more difficult chord, Bm. Plus, we'll discuss three different types of sheet music, both online and printed versions. You'll finish this chapter with some rhythm chart examples now in your third key!

The Key of D

Like the last chapter, we are learning a new key. The good news again is that you already know some of the relative chords. The new key is D. You know D (which is now the root or fundamental chord), Em, and G. You'll need the chords A and Bm to complete the important chords for this key.

A Chord

To build an A chord you'll only need two fingers. First, place your middle (2) finger onto the second fret of the fourth [G] string. Last, add your index (1) finger to the first fret of the third [C] string. Strum all four strings leaving the second [E] and first [A] strings open.

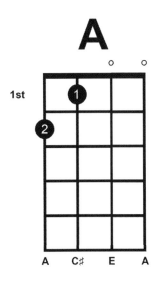

Bm Chord

The Bm chord is certainly the toughest chord to learn in this book. But it is doable! This is also the only chord with a barre. A barre means that a single finger will lay across more than one fret and string thus holding the strings down to produce the necessary notes.

Build Bm by first placing your ring (3) finger onto the fourth fret of the fourth [G] string. Now, you'll want to barre the second fret of the remaining strings with your index (1) finger. Begin by pressing down the third [C] string. Then, lay down across the remaining two strings. Pluck each of the barred strings to confirm you have solid sounding notes. You don't want any buzzing sound. That would mean that your contact with the second fret of that note's string is not fully in place or held firmly. Strum across all four strings to make Bm.

This chord will take extra effort and practice. Days one and two may be frustrating to you. Take your time and come back to Bm each day until it sounds right. You can do this!

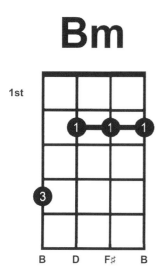

Chord Charts

It's important that as a musician–not just a ukulele player, but as a musician–that you learn how to read sheet music. The most basic way you'll see music is the chords-over-words method called chord charts. This is where you'll find a chord written directly over top of the lyric being sung. You only make a chord transition when the words change. This is the easiest form of "sheet music" to create because it only takes a word processor, like Microsoft Word™, to create. Unfortunately, this is the least accurate form. The placement of the chords can sometimes appear arbitrary. Also, what about the times when the singer isn't singing, like in an intro or turnaround? Most songs you search for online will show with results for chord charts.

Uke Tablature (Tabs)

When searching the Internet, you'll find lots of *ukulele tabs* (or ukulele tablature). Similar to chords-over-words charts, uke tabs are easily made in word processors. They look a bit like sheet music, but the lines going across your page or screen represent strings. Therefore you'll see four lines. On those lines, you'll find numbers. Each number represents a fret to be pressed down. For example (0003) is the C chord you've learned. What this doesn't tell you is when to play the C or, in the case of a chord you don't know, which finger to put on the designated frets. Ukulele tabs are most helpful once you've gotten your feet wet with the uke and want to learn a specific part that someone has transcribed.

Sheet Music and Lead Sheets

Sheet music, or staff music, is the oldest form of written music and has the highest accuracy of any transcription method. Beethoven used sheet music. Bono uses sheet music. Sheet music can be complicated, like a Bach piece, or it can be simple. Most worship or pop music that you'll purchase is written in a simple form of sheet music, called a *lead sheet*. You'll see rhythm notes, chords, and standard notes with the lyrics written below them. There are measure indications so you'll know where a measure begins and ends. There are also indications such as dynamic cues (louder/softer) and tempo cues (beats per minute and ritardando (rit.)). Sheet music is typically created by professionals, so it costs money. There are several resources (searchable on Google) that will provide free sheet music each week.

Nashville Numbers System

The Nashville numbers system is the final form of sheet music to know about. The basic premise is that the tonic chord is your "1 chord", then your respective chords get assigned a number based on where they sit in the scale. In the key of "D", for example, the 1 chord is D, the 2m chord is an Em, the 4 chord is G, and so on. The difficulty with this type of notation is that the player has to "really know his numbers", as they say. You have to know which chords do and do not belong in the key of "D". You also have to do math in your head as the chords change, which isn't easily done on the fly. I do recommend trying to learn this type of notation, but leave it for as you progress!

Rhythm chart examples using the D, Em, Bm, and A chords

First, we'll play a chord progression in the key of D using our new A chord. Play this with alternating up and down strums.

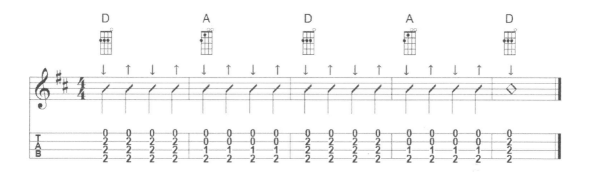

Second, let's use a similar progression but use our new Bm. Continue to play this with alternating up and down strums.

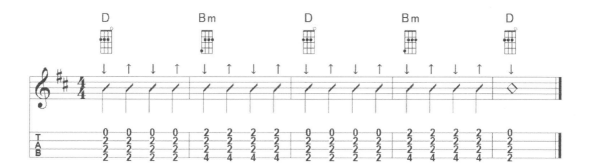

Now, let's play a chord progression using the main chords in the key of D.

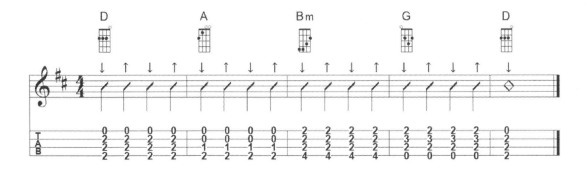

This last exercise uses all chords in the key of D but moves quickly between each one. Since this is the final exercise for this book, test yourself by using alternating up and down strums while playing this quick-moving progression. You can do it!

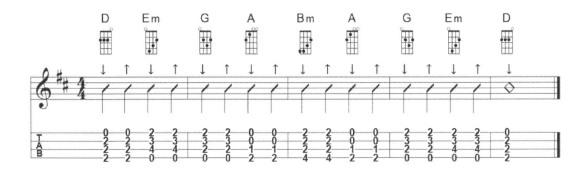

Final Greetings

You've made it!

You now know nine chords on the ukulele! Plus, you can play in three important keys: C, G, and D. With your capo, you can play in any key too! This is a big day! In fact, this has been an incredible six weeks. Well done!

Now it's time to consider when you should begin the guitar. Many of the techniques and a few of the chord shapes you've already learned will transition easily to the guitar. My recommendation is that you wait until your hands are large enough to hold a standard size guitar. Three quarter and child-size guitars exist but are not typically built to the same quality standard as a full-size guitar. I recommend waiting until your hands are big enough to play the full-size and you can hold the guitar properly while standing.

Whether you are ready to move to the guitar or are waiting until the timing is right, below are some recommended resources to help you along the way. Since you have been successful with this book, consider using some of my other books to continue your success. It's been a privilege to have helped you thus far. Let's keep going!

Recommended Resources

Worship Guitar In Six Weeks

Worship Guitar In Six Weeks is a perfect primer for anyone interested in joining a worship team as a rhythm guitar player. This is the best book for those coming from this book as a beginner ukulele player. The premise is that you need only a few quick tools to learn before you have enough knowledge and skill to play with a group. It teaches the parts that make up the guitar, a few important chords, how to strum, and a bit more. I recommend this book for the beginner. The pacing is perfect!

42 Guitar Chords Everyone Should Know

Using *42 Guitar Chords Everyone Should Know*, you'll take a deeper dive into how guitar chords relate one to another. You'll learn how to move quickly between G to D to Em to Cadd9–each chord important for the key of G. *42 Chords* is a great next step after *Worship Guitar In Six Weeks*.

Fast Guitar Chord Transitions

One of the neatest books I've ever worked on is *Fast Guitar Chord Transitions*. Most guitar manuals will show you how to play chords. This includes finger placement, which strings to strum, and so on. But, one overlooked aspect of the guitar is that transitioning between chords is as important as knowing the chords themselves. In *Fast Guitar Chord Transitions*, I walk a guitarist through the steps of transitioning all of the most popular chord moves you'll need to know. The book is arranged based on the key of a song in which you may be playing. It's worth every penny!

Guitar Secrets Revealed

Guitar Secrets Revealed is a book for the intermediate player looking for professional level insights. Use this manual to get inside the mind of the pro. Find out how they think. You'll learn practicable–actionable–music theory that can be implemented today. Plus, find out how to use more unique guitar chord shapes that work like inversions of basic chords. All in all, this book takes a guitar player to the next level–maybe even up two levels!

BONUS: Piano Chords One and Two

While the scope of the book in your hands is for ukulele players, I cannot highly recommend enough my *Piano Authority Series* of books: *Piano Chords One* and *Two*. Quickly translate everything that you know about ukulele chords to the piano. You'd be amazed at how much transfers! Written much like a ukulele manual, you'll learn the most important chords to play on the piano and how to play all the different versions of them. If you've ever longed to be able to play through songs on the piano and accompany yourself, these two books will help you do that. Grab a copy of each and see what you can accomplish!

Appendix

Chord Diagram

Each chord in this book has a unique diagram. There are several parts to each one. Refer back to this section as you need to when working through this manual.

Chord Diagram Explained

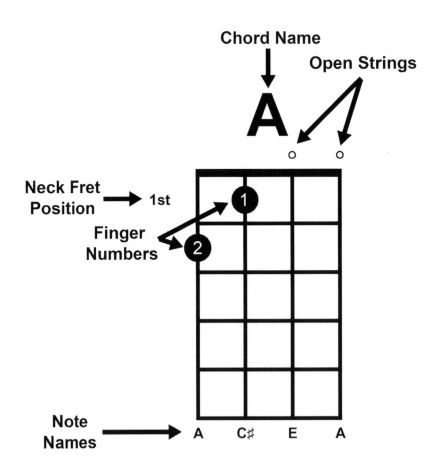

Chord Name

This section details the name of the chord. This may include a chord suffix, like E<u>m</u> where the "m" is at the end and is a modifier.

Open String

An open string is a ukulele string played with no finger touching it. The note name is the string's name. For example, if you play the open third and fourth strings, like in this A chord example, the open notes played on the second [E] string is an "E" and the first [A] string is an "A". An open string will always have an "o" above the string.

Muted String

A muted string is one that is either being muted by a neighboring finger or intentionally not being played with the right, strumming hand. A muted string will always have an "x" above the string.

Neck Fret Position

The neck fret position number is important to always notice when reviewing a chord diagram. That number signifies the starting position of your fingers on the neck. It can go as high as the last fret on the upper part of your ukulele neck. If you see a "1st" denotation, then the chord is played in the open position at the beginning of the neck. "1st" is the *home base* position on the uke. Everything else is related to that home base position.

Finger Numbers

While you could use nicknames for each finger on your left hand (like your index finger, pinky, etc.) most teachers will use numbers per finger. Using numbers allows for quick reference for chord diagrams and transitioning.

Here is how each finger of the left hand is noted in this book. The index finger is (1). Your middle finger is (2), ring finger is (3), and pinky finger is (4). I label the thumb (T). While you will not get into any thumb playing in this book, you may as you improve in your skills moving on to further chording. Note: left-handed players will use the opposite hand, making each of the labels above true for the *right hand* rather than the left.

Note Names

Below each chord diagram are the note names being played per string. Please notice that these are <u>not</u> the root names of the strings. Rather, these are the notes being played after fretting the chord. Some of the notes will be the open string notes, but only when there is no finger needed for that particular string in the chord. When a string is being omitted or muted, no note name will be present.

About The Author

Why so many people learn music from Micah

The best instructors teach to the student, not to the curriculum. The curriculum serves as a vehicle for learning. It's a tool of sorts. One of the best parts of teaching music lessons–in this case, ukelele–is the ability to help a student learn at just the right pace. I've found that my job as an educator is to always be encouraging my students to take one step more than he or she may not have taken on their own. The only thing to sort out is at which pace you perform best.

I've been teaching guitar, ukulele, and piano courses for more than ten years. In fact, that's why I've written five books for guitar, one for ukulele, and two for piano to date. My emphasis has always been, and will likely always be, in commercial music. While I think classical music is worth studying, I always find myself improvising over the original melodies–even those of the greats, like Beethoven, Brahms, or Bach. It's human nature to explore or be curious and I love teaching with the mindset that the music greats of the past are like proven guides. They shouldn't always be copied, but rather those from whom to learn.

Living twenty-five miles from downtown Nashville, TN has provided me and my family privileges in music that I'm certain are not given in every town. You can't throw a stone in Nashville without hitting someone who is personally or has a family member in the music industry. Not one of us takes the Grand Ole Opry backstage tour because we all plan to be there as a music artist someday. Even if we sing and play music for Jesus as Christian or worship artists, we still likely won't spend the time or money for that tour. We plan to perform on that ageless circle that lands center-stage someday ourselves.

My wife of more than ten years is wonderful and my greatest joy.

Micah Brooks

We have four kids who keep us very busy and quite exhausted! We also keep two Yorkshire Terrier dogs who I'm sure my wife would give away for less than the price of two movie tickets. I love them though. Plus, we just got an all-black labradoodle.

It's an honor to help you work toward your ukelele goals. These new chords may unlock creativity in you that has been buried deep within for years. It's time to let it out!

Blessings,

-Micah Brooks
www.micahbrooks.com
Find me on Facebook, Twitter, LinkedIn,
Instagram, and Amazon.com

Connect With Micah Brooks

Signup for Micah Brooks emails to stay up to date

Subscribe to the Micah Brooks Company "Stay Connected" email list for the latest book releases. This email list is always free and intended to deliver high-value content to your inbox. Visit the link below to signup.

www.micahbrooks.com

Contact Micah

Email Micah Brooks at micahbrooks.com/contact. I want to know who you are. It's my privilege to respond to your emails personally. Please feel free to connect.

Please share this book with your friends

If you would like to share your thanks for this book, the best thing you can do is to tell a friend about *Ukulele In Six Weeks* or buy them a copy. You can also show your appreciation for this book by leaving a five-star review on Amazon:

www.amazon.com

Follow Micah Brooks:

Facebook, Twitter, LinkedIn, and Instagram
Amazon: amazon.com/author/micahbrooks

If you have trouble connecting to any of these social media accounts, please visit www.micahbrooks.com.

Micah Brooks

Sing to him a new song;
play skillfully, and shout for joy.

Psalm 33:3 (NIV)

Micah Brooks

Printed in Great Britain
by Amazon